D1545323

SPACE TECH

MARS ROVERS

by ALLAN MOREY

EPIC

BELLWETHER MEDIA • MINNEAPOLIS, MN

EPIC BOOKS are no ordinary books. They burst with intense action, high-speed heroics, and shadows of the unknown. Are you ready for an Epic adventure?

This edition first published in 2018 by Bellwether Media, Inc.

No part of this publication may be reproduced in whole or in part without written permission of the publisher. For information regarding permission, write to Bellwether Media, Inc., Attention: Permissions Department, 5357 Penn Avenue South, Minneapolis, MN 55419.

Library of Congress Cataloging-in-Publication Data

Names: Morey, Allan.
Title: Mars Rovers / by Allan Morey.
Description: Minneapolis, MN : Bellwether Media, Inc., 2018. | Series: Epic. Space Tech | Audience: Age 7-12. | Includes bibliographical references and index.
Identifiers: LCCN 2016057240 (print) | LCCN 2017010614 (ebook) | ISBN 9781626177031 (hardcover : alk. paper) | ISBN 9781681034331 (ebook) | ISBN 9781618912862 (paperback : alk. paper)
Subjects: LCSH: Roving vehicles (Astronautics)–Juvenile literature. | Mars (Planet)–Exploration–Juvenile literature. | Mars probes–Juvenile literature.
Classification: LCC TL475 .M67 2018 (print) | LCC TL475 (ebook) | DDC 629.2/95099923-dc23
LC record available at https://lccn.loc.gov/2016057240

Editor: Nathan Sommer   Designer: Steve Porter

Printed in the United States of America, North Mankato, MN.

TABLE OF CONTENTS

MARS ROVER AT WORK!

A **spacecraft** nears the planet Mars. It carries the Curiosity **rover**. The spacecraft drops near the surface. Then a crane lowers Curiosity. Its landing is a success! This new Mars rover is ready to explore.

Curiosity

ALL IN A NAME!

"Rover" also means a person who wanders around.

WHAT ARE MARS ROVERS?

Mars rovers are machines sent to Mars. This planet is too far away for humans to reach right now. Rovers are sent instead. The machines move around the planet and study it for humans.

NASA engineers with three types of Mars rovers

Curiosity

Sojourner

RED PLANET!

Mars is often called the "Red Planet." Its soil often looks red.

soil sample
from Mars

Rovers collect rocks and soil.
They take pictures and try to find
signs of water. They also study
the planet's **atmosphere**. Their
findings are then sent back to Earth.

PARTS OF MARS ROVERS

Rovers are built to survive on Mars. They have thick wheels. These help rovers climb over the rocky surface. **Solar panels** usually power rovers.

solar panel

WHEELS GO ROUND!

Rovers were the first machines with wheels used on a planet other than Earth.

Rovers have many tools needed to study Mars. Robotic arms drill into rocks and scrape soil for **samples**. Cameras on the machines take pictures. Rovers use **antennae** to send and receive messages.

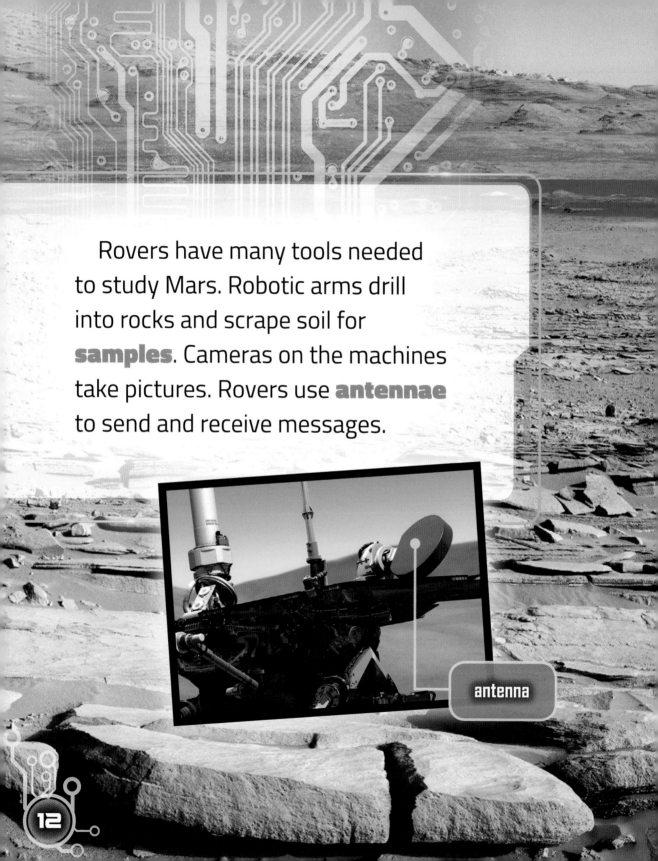

antenna

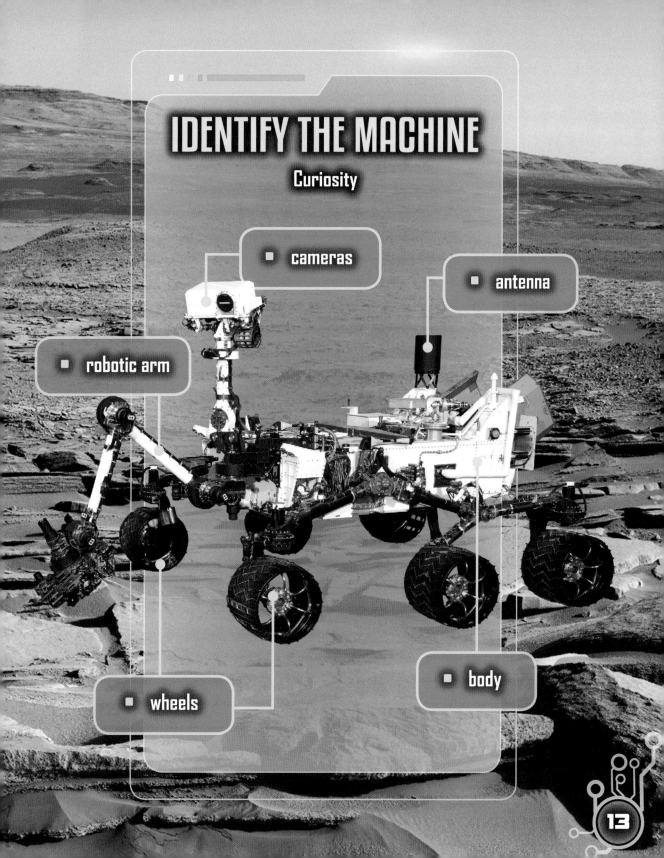

IDENTIFY THE MACHINE
Curiosity

cameras

antenna

robotic arm

wheels

body

MARS ROVER MISSIONS

In the 1970s, the **Soviet Union** sent the first rovers to Mars. They traveled on the Mars 2 and Mars 3 spacecraft. Mars 2 crash-landed. Mars 3 stopped working soon after reaching the planet. Both **missions** failed.

Mars 3

Mars 3
orbiter

Sojourner

Sojourner became the first rover to land and work on Mars. It showed **NASA** that it was possible to reach and explore the planet. Two more rovers landed on Mars in 2004. They discovered the planet once had water!

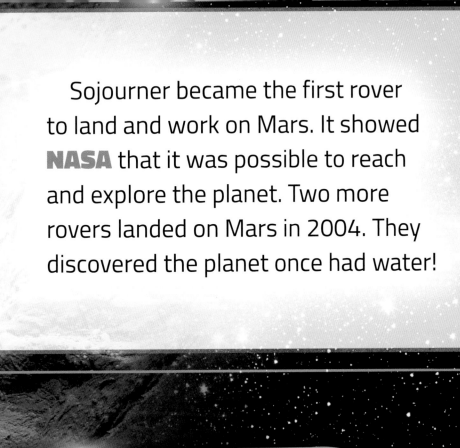

JUST LIKE HOME!

Mars is like Earth in many ways. Clouds fill its sky. Seasons change as it circles the sun.

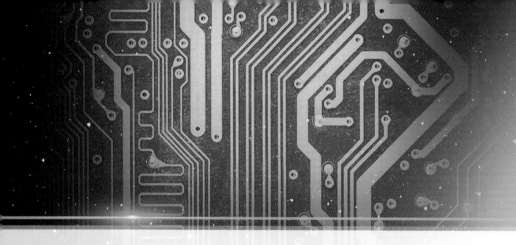

Curiosity is the most recent rover to land on Mars. One of its missions is to study the planet's weather. It is also trying to discover if Mars once had life. Future rovers might study if people can live on the planet. Thanks to rovers, humans may one day step foot on Mars!

Curiosity

GOAL GETTERS!

NASA's goal is to send humans to Mars in the 2030s.

CURIOSITY SPECS

Curiosity current location:
area around Mount Sharp,
Gale Crater

NAME: CURIOSITY
Mars Science Laboratory

- length: 10 feet (3 meters)
- height: 7 feet (2.1 meters)

- mission: to see if life once existed on Mars and to study the planet's weather
- first time in space: 2011
- distance traveled: 660 feet (201 meters) per day

- width: 9 feet (2.7 meters)

21

GLOSSARY

antennae—devices used for sending and receiving information

atmosphere—the gases that surround a planet

missions—tasks or jobs

NASA—National Aeronautics and Space Administration; NASA is a U.S. government agency responsible for space travel and exploration.

rover—a vehicle that explores surfaces outside of Earth

samples—small amounts that stand for the whole

solar panels—devices that collect sunlight and turn it into energy

Soviet Union—a former country in eastern Europe and western Asia made up of 15 smaller republics or states

spacecraft—any vehicle used to travel in outer space

TO LEARN MORE

AT THE LIBRARY

Kortenkamp, Steve. *Mars Exploration Rovers*. North Mankato, Minn.: Capstone Press, 2017.

Payment, Simone. *Mars*. New York, N.Y.: Rosen Educational Publishing, 2017.

VanVoorst, Jenny Fretland. *Rovers*. Minneapolis, Minn.: Pogo, 2017.

ON THE WEB
Learning more about Mars rovers is as easy as 1, 2, 3.

1. Go to www.factsurfer.com.

2. Enter "Mars rovers" into the search box.

3. Click the "Surf" button and you will see a list of related web sites.

With factsurfer.com, finding more information is just a click away.

WWW.FACTSURFER.COM

INDEX

The images in this book are reproduced through the courtesy of: alex7370, front cover (rocks); Triff, front cover (rover); Aphelleon, pp. 2-3; NASA, pp. 4 (rover), 4-5, 6-7, 8 (rover), 8-9 (Mars surface), 9 (soil sample), 10-13 (all), 14 (lander), 18-19 (rover), 20-21 (all); MarcelClemens, p. 5 (Moon-FunFact); Odishev, p. 5 (person-FunFact); Tristan3D, p. 8 (Mars); kvsan, pp. 14-15 (Mars); The Powerhouse Museum, p. 15 (orbiter); Konstantin Kowarsch/ Dreamstime, pp. 16-17; Orlando Florin Rosu/ Dreamstime, p. 17 (Mars/Earth-FunFact); Moviestore collection Ltd/ Alamy, p. 19 (Matt Damon).